This Communication Book
Belongs To:

_____

How to Use This Book?

Understanding Non-Verbal Communication Cards

Non-verbal communication cards, often referred to as Picture Exchange Communication Systems (PECS), comprise a set of visual aids featuring images or symbols representing various concepts, actions, and objects. These cards provide individuals with Autism Spectrum Disorder (ASD) with an alternative means of communication, bypassing the barriers associated with verbal expression.

Who Can Benefit from Non-Verbal Communication Cards

- For individuals with autism or related conditions.
- For individuals who experience sensory overload or anxiety in social situations. By using the cards to communicate their feelings, they may feel more comfortable and less overwhelmed.
- Caregivers and educators who work with individuals with ASD.

Benefits of Non-Verbal Communication Cards

♥ Enhance Understanding:

Visual aids are often more accessible and comprehensible for individuals with ASD, as they rely on concrete representations rather than abstract language. Non-verbal communication cards aid in comprehension, enabling individuals to grasp concepts and instructions more readily.

♥ Promoting Independence:

By equipping individuals with ASD with non-verbal communication cards, caregivers and educators foster independence and autonomy. These tools empower individuals to make choices, express preferences, and navigate their environments with confidence.

♥ Reducing Anxiety:

The predictability and clarity offered by these visual cards can alleviate anxiety and stress in individuals with ASD. Having a visual means of communication provides a sense of security and control, reducing the uncertainty often associated with verbal interactions.

How to Use Non-Verbal Communication Cards

1. Introduction and Familiarization: Introduce the individual to the non-verbal communication cards, ensuring they understand the meaning of each symbol or image.
2. Practice and Reinforcement: Engage in regular practice sessions to reinforce the use of non-verbal communication cards. Encourage them to select cards to express their needs, desires, or emotions.
3. Integration into Daily Routine: Incorporate non-verbal communication cards into daily activities and routines. Use them during meal times, transitions, and social interactions to promote consistent usage.

4. Individualized Approach: Tailor the selection of non-verbal communication cards to the their preferences and needs. Add your own picture in the empty cards section.

5. Encouragement and Positive Reinforcement: Give praise and encouragement for using non-verbal communication cards effectively. Reinforce their efforts with positive feedback and rewards to motivate continued progress.

Tips for Effective Communication

1. Patience and Understanding: Approach communication with patience and empathy, understanding that individuals with ASD may require additional time to process information and respond.

2. Respect Personal Space: Respect the individual's personal space and boundaries, allowing them to communicate at their own pace and comfort level.

3. Clear and Simple Language: When using verbal communication alongside non-verbal communication cards, employ clear and simple language to enhance comprehension.

4. Use Visual Cues: Incorporate visual cues and gestures to supplement verbal and non-verbal communication, providing additional support and context.

5. Encourage Self-Advocacy: Foster self-advocacy skills by encouraging the individual to initiate communication using non-verbal communication cards and advocate for their needs and preferences.

Feelings

Happy	Sad	Mad
Excited	Scared	Surprised
Tired	Hot	Cold
Thirsty	Hungry	Sick

Communication

Communication

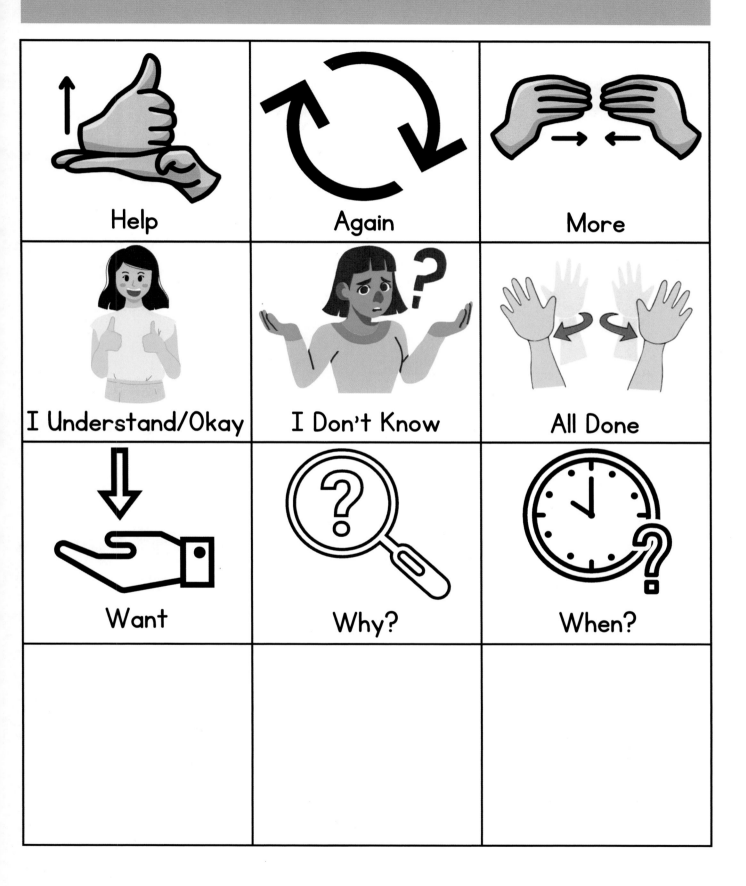

Help	Again	More
I Understand/Okay	I Don't Know	All Done
Want	Why?	When?

Preposition

Inside	Outside	Under
Above	Between	Across
Through	In Front of	Around
Up	Down	Far

Personal Needs

Take A Shower

Take A Bath

Diaper Change

Get Dressed

Put on a Coat

Put on Shoes

Go Potty

Brush Teeth

Drink A Bottle

Bedtime

Playtime

Eat A Meal

Personal Needs

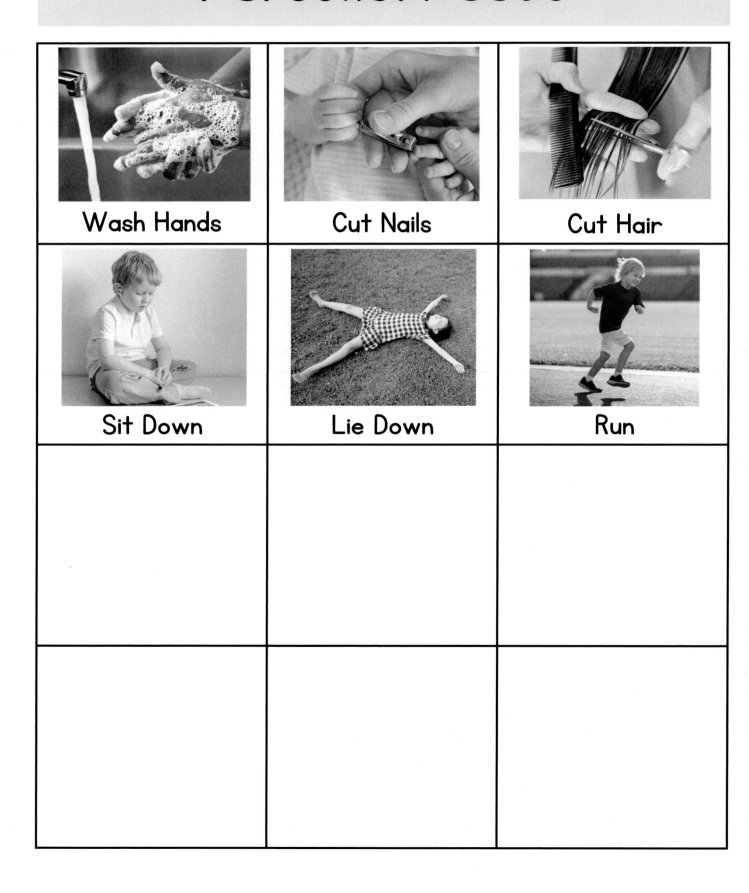

| Wash Hands | Cut Nails | Cut Hair |
| Sit Down | Lie Down | Run |

Family

Insert your family member pictures here

Items

Phones	Tablet	Remote
Glasses	Pencil	Eraser
Toilet	Toilet Paper	Nappy
Wipes	Shirt	Pants

Items

Play Dough	Blocks	Stuffed Animal
Toy Cars	Crayons	Puzzle
Bike	Helmet	Balls

Routines

Alarm	Wake Up	Make the Bed
Brush Teeth	Get Dressed	Have Breakfast
Get Bag Ready	Put Shoes On	Go Outside
Say Bye	Car	School Bus

Routines

Study/Read Books

Exercise

Lunch Time

Go For A Walk

Go Home

Wash Hands

Relax

Play Time

Watch TV

Tablet

Crafts

Coloring

Routines

Play With Ball	Dance	Toys
Tidy Up	Homework	Quiet Time
Dinner Time	Put On Pajamas	Story Time
Bedtime		

Places

Cinema	Park	Playground
Grocery Shopping	School	Swimming Pool
Restaurant	Police Station	Fire Station

Food

Chicken	Meat	Fish
Egg	Hard Boiled Egg	Fried Egg
Scrambled Egg	Toasted Bread	Sandwich
Pancakes	Hamburger	Pizza

Food

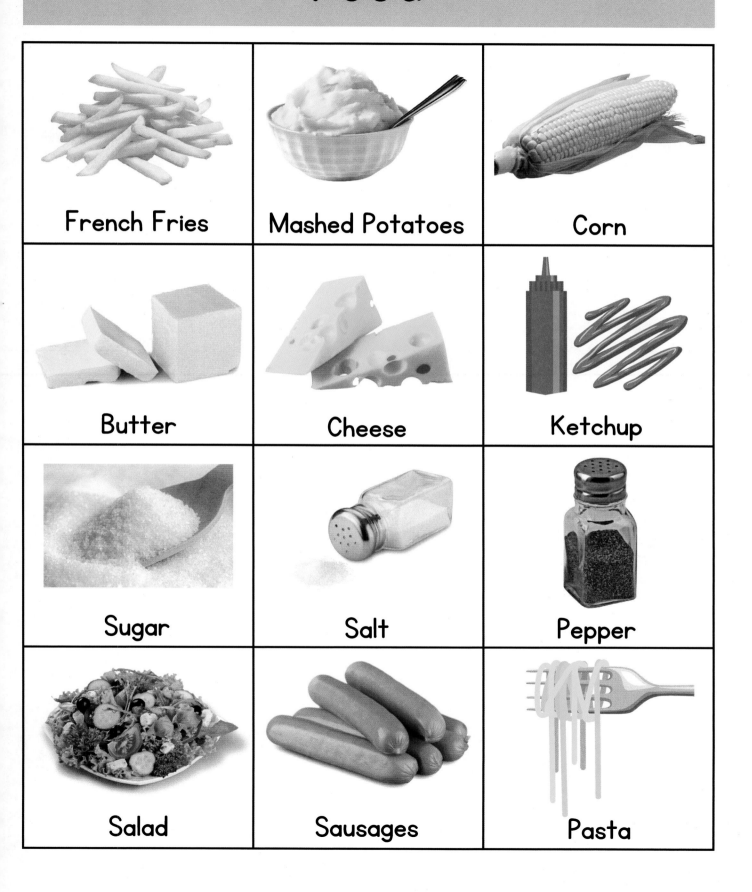

French Fries

Mashed Potatoes

Corn

Butter

Cheese

Ketchup

Sugar

Salt

Pepper

Salad

Sausages

Pasta

Food

Cupcake	Muffin	Cookies
Ice Cream	Oatmeal	Cracker

Fruits and Drinks

Water

Milk

Juice

Apple

Banana

Orange

Apple

Blueberries

Grapes

Lemon

Watermelon

Mango

Body Parts

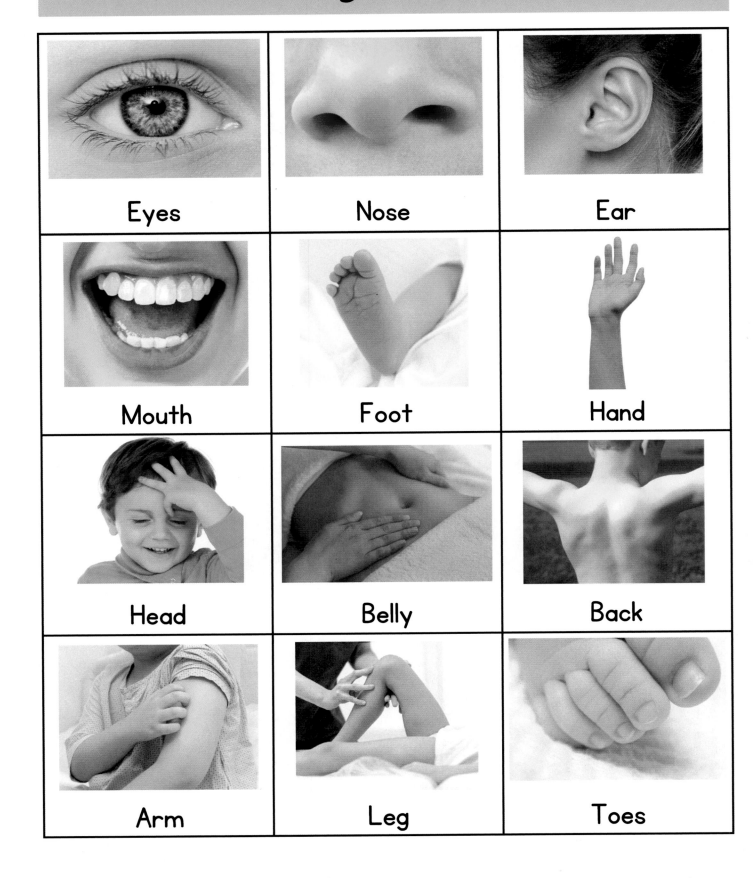

Eyes	Nose	Ear
Mouth	Foot	Hand
Head	Belly	Back
Arm	Leg	Toes

Pain Scale

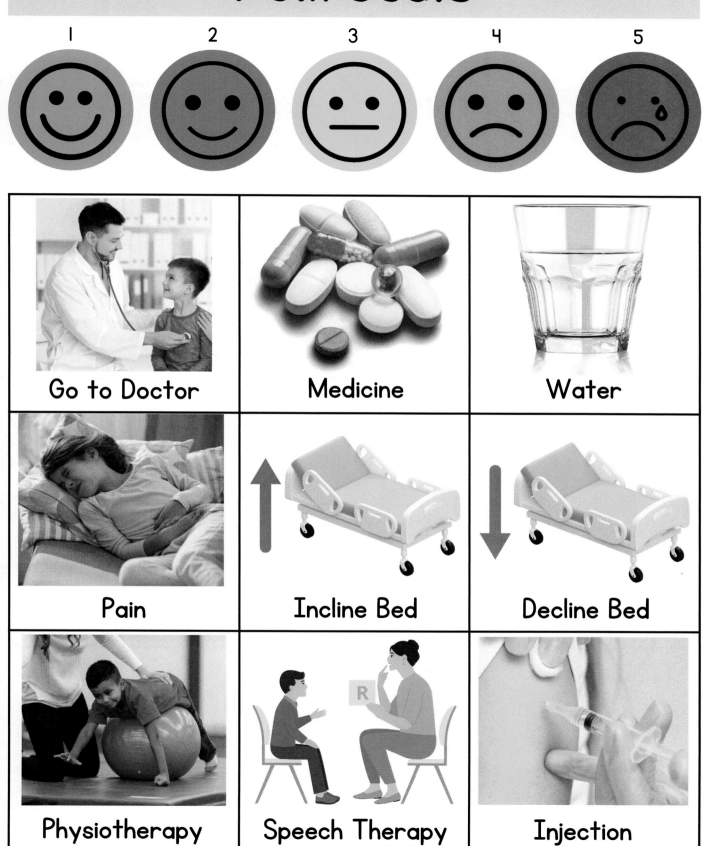

Calm Down Strategies

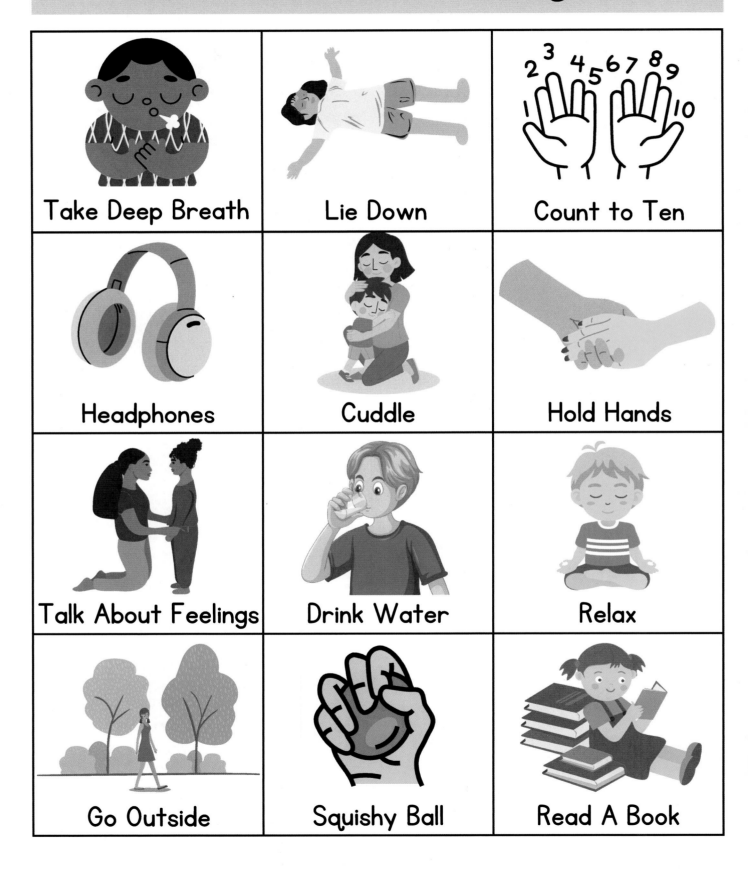

Take Deep Breath	Lie Down	Count to Ten
Headphones	Cuddle	Hold Hands
Talk About Feelings	Drink Water	Relax
Go Outside	Squishy Ball	Read A Book

Behavior

Add your own pictures here

Made in the USA
Las Vegas, NV
30 November 2024